The World of Work

Choosing a Career as a Paramedic

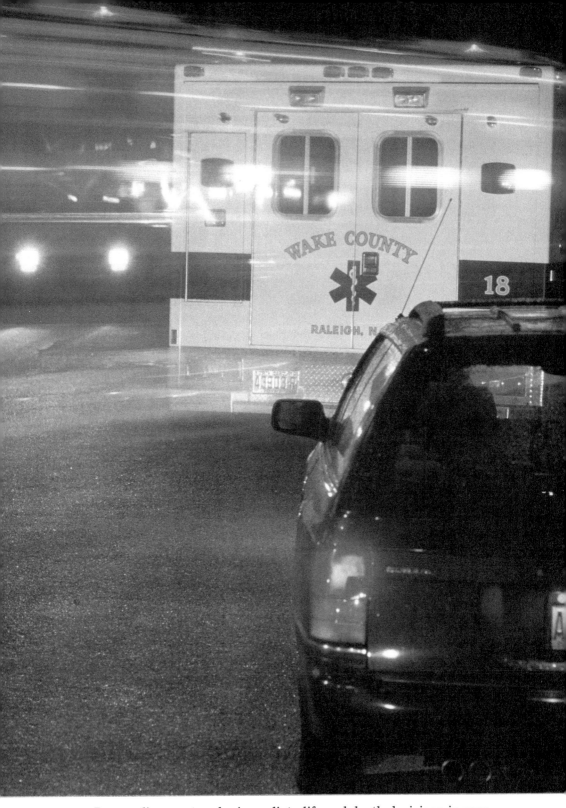

Paramedics must make immediate life-and-death decisions in very chaotic circumstances.

The World of Work

Choosing a Career as a Paramedic

Sandra and Owen Giddens

The Rosen Publishing Group, Inc.
New York

*To Justine and Kyle, and thank you to the brave paramedics
in Florida and in Toronto.*

Published in 1997, 2000 by The Rosen Publishing Group, Inc.
29 East 21st Street, New York, NY 10010

Revised Edition 2000

Library of Congress Cataloging-in-Publication Data

Giddens, Sandra.
    Choosing a career as a paramedic / Sandra and Owen Giddens.
        p. cm.—(The world of work)
    Includes bibliographical references and index.
    Summary: Discusses the work performed by paramedics and the skills and
training needed to prepare for a career in this field.
    ISBN 0-8239-3244-3 (lib. bdg. : alk. paper)
        1. Emergency medical technicians—Vocational Guidance—Juvenile
    literature. [1. Emergency medical technicians—Vocational Guidance.
    2. Vocational Guidance.] I. Giddens, Owen. II. Title. III. World of work
    (New York, NY).

RC86.5 .G53 2000
610.69'53'023—dc21
                                                                99-058621

Manufactured in the United States of America

Contents

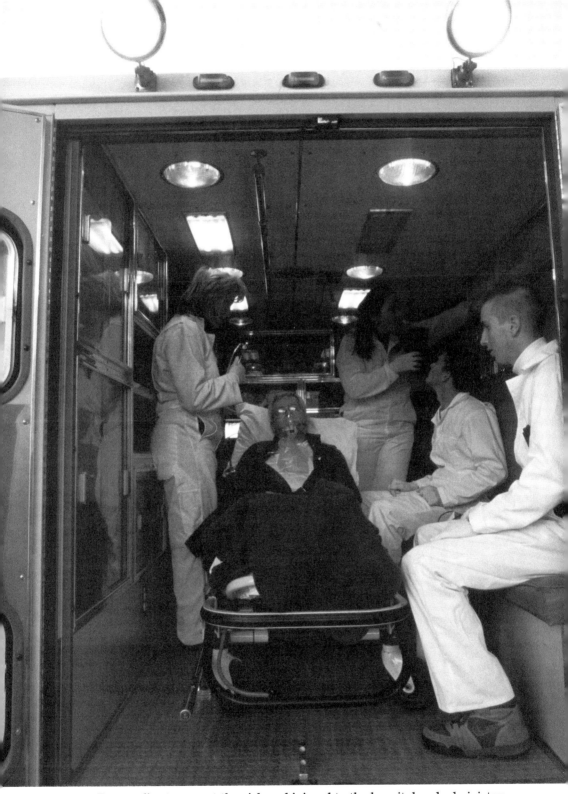

Paramedics transport the sick and injured to the hospital and administer emergency medical treatment on the way there.

Introduction

The high-pitched siren of the ambulance pierces the air. Cars pull over to make way for its passage. People stop and stare. The ambulance evokes many emotions. There is fascination, curiosity, and sometimes a feeling of fear in people's minds as the ambulance zooms by. Where is it going, and who is inside? Has there been an accident? Will the person live or die? Could the emergency be in my neighborhood or at my house?

The workers inside the ambulance are called paramedics. These specially trained men and women are there to do a multitude of jobs. Not only do they transport the sick and injured to the hospital, but they administer emergency medical treatment so that those people will still be alive when they get there. They must make quick and accurate appraisals of a patient's condition and then respond swiftly with the right treatment. They must know how to restore a heartbeat and how to stop severe bleeding.

They must recognize the symptoms of a drug overdose or a severe asthma attack. They must get their patients to the hospital quickly, and they must accurately report all that they've observed to the doctors.

The paramedic-equipped ambulance offers the sick and injured a lot more than just a trip to the hospital. Thousands of lives are saved every day by the decisions and actions of paramedics.

So what is it like to be a paramedic? What is it like to be first on the scene of an accident, miraculously saving lives? Does it produce an adrenaline rush? Or is there more to this occupation than what is seen on television and in the movies? Who are the paramedics and what are their feelings toward their jobs? In this book we will meet a number of paramedics. Through their eyes we will discover what the work is really like, how one qualifies and trains for such work, and what qualities make a good paramedic. This is a tough, fast-paced, and pressured type of work, in which the price of mistakes is very high, but the reward— saving lives—is unlike any reward that any other job can give you.

What Is a Paramedic? 1

A paramedic is a worker who administers prehospital emergency medical care and life-support services to the sick and injured. When you have a medical emergency, paramedics are your first face-to-face contact with the medical profession. Paramedics are not doctors, but they are trained to recognize and respond to the most basic kinds of trauma or physical injury. Paramedics do not cure illnesses or repair bodily injuries. Their function is to stabilize patients, to make sure that their hearts are pumping, that they are still breathing, and that they are not bleeding badly or suffering from shock. Then they can be safely transported by ambulance, helicopter, or boat to hospitals or other medical facilities for further care. Paramedics are employed by public and private ambulance services and hospitals. They can also be part of fire and rescue services, government agencies, or private companies.

One of the first duties of a paramedic is

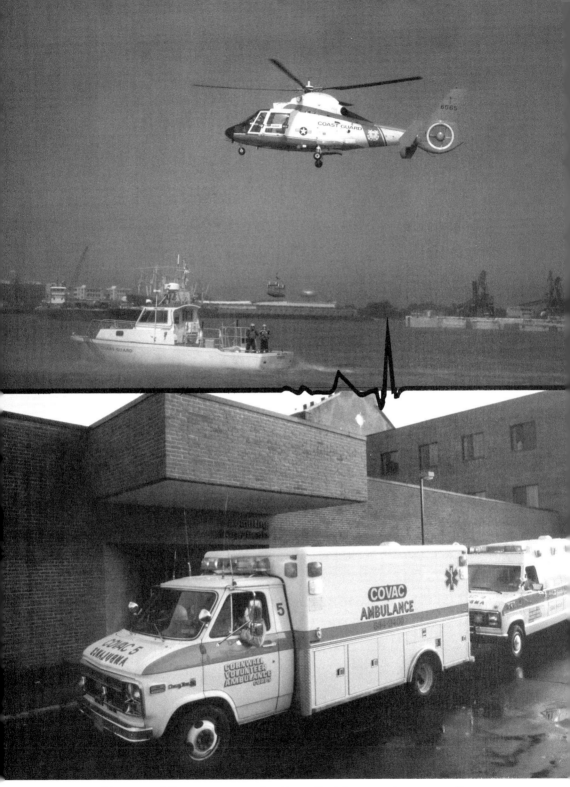

Because of the emergency situations the job presents, paramedics are often licensed to drive an ambulance, a plane, a helicopter, or a boat.

to assess the extent of the injuries of a victim of trauma or the seriousness of someone's illness. Paramedics will be involved in many different types of situations and must quickly decide what kind of emergency medical treatment is needed. The injured or sick may have a multitude of medical difficulties that the paramedic must immediately attend to, such as respiratory distress, a drug overdose, poisoning, lacerations, fractures, or a heart attack. Paramedics must even be prepared to assist a woman giving birth. Their patients may also have minor injuries or ailments that don't require transport to the hospital but that must be dealt with all the same. In many instances, the initial emergency care rendered by paramedics will be the deciding factor between temporary or permanent disability, a brief confinement or prolonged hospitalization, or even between life and death.

The responsibilities of paramedics vary from state to state in the United States and from province to province in Canada. Throughout North America, all paramedics are trained to administer CPR (cardiopulmonary resuscitation), give oxygen, bandage wounds, and treat fractures with splints. They can also insert and maintain IV (intravenous) tubes, defibrillate (stimulate through electric shock) heart attack victims, and administer medications. Paramedics are specially licensed to drive an ambulance, a plane, a helicopter, or a boat. From their vehicles, they transport their patients to hospitals or other medical facilities. At the hospital, their patients will be looked after by medical personnel and receive further treatment.

Part of the paramedic's job is to document all that he or she observes, to make an accurate description of the extent and nature of injuries or symptoms, and to write up a complete report of the emergency procedures that were undertaken and the medicines administered. This is done through both portable computers and information sheets. Recording is a vital part of the paramedic's day-to-day activities. This information provides emergency room doctors with a head start in diagnosing problems and selecting treatments with a minimum loss of time. If, for example, paramedics have to give medication, they record it and inform the

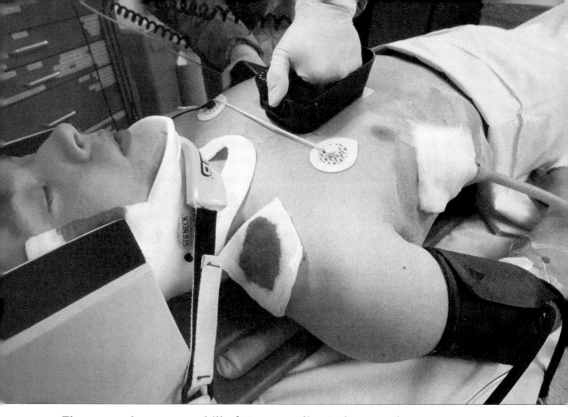

There are always new skills for paramedics to learn and new pieces of medical equipment to master, such as the defibrillator.

medical facility of the exact dose and the time administered.

Paramedics are also required to see that their ambulances and equipment are well maintained and in excellent working order at all times. It is essential that they have up-to-date equipment and that they are fully supplied before leaving on an emergency call. Their ambulances are well organized so that they know where everything is kept and can reach things quickly in an emergency. They have been trained to operate all the medical equipment inside the ambulance, as well as to administer drugs. Paramedics have

13

to be clearheaded and in complete control throughout an emergency situation.

The paramedic's job is always evolving. There are always new skills to learn and new pieces of medical equipment to master. Every emergency call is an opportunity to figure out better and faster ways of working. Many paramedics train or act as mentors to other paramedic workers in their unit or squad.

An important part of the paramedic's role is educating the public to help in the prevention of further injuries. Paramedics often conduct public education campaigns on how to recognize and deal with the symptoms of heat exposure, how to practice safety in the water, or the importance of having carbon monoxide detectors in cars. These kinds of preventive programs lead to fewer injuries and fewer deaths in the community.

From the Past to the Present

Before the 1960s, ambulance fleets were either under the management of hospitals or were privately owned. Their equipment consisted solely of simple first-aid materials like bandages and splints. Most often a driver and a helper were the occupants of the ambulance. The helper was trained to treat only the simplest of medical emergencies. At times, doctors rode in the ambulances, but this was not typical. The ambulance was little more than a shuttle to get you to the hospital. A patient's first encounter with trained medical personnel took place in the emergency room, and not before, if he or she was lucky enough to make it that far. Thousands died needlessly on the way to the hospital for lack of timely and proper treatment.

The 1960s saw the introduction of the "hospital on wheels" concept. These new ambulances were crewed by people with some medical training. They could give medications and oxygen, and if the patient's heart had stopped beating, they carried defibrillators to revive the victim with electric shocks. By the late 1960s, most states in the United States required anyone transporting sick or injured people to undergo training and become a certified EMT (emergency medical technician). These EMTs provided basic life support to their patients, but it still was not enough to save many lives. In the 1970s, programs were started to train

New York City's Emergency Medical Service

In the early 1970s, New York City faced a crisis in its emergency medical service. More and more hospitals were choosing not to participate in the city's EMS system, decreasing the number of available ambulances, while the number of emergency responses began to exceed 400,000 a year. Ambulance crews consisted of a motor vehicle operator (MVO) and an emergency medical technician (EMT). The MVO did nothing but drive the ambulance, and only the EMT had medical training.

In 1973, the newly created Health and Hospitals Corporation decided to cross-train all ambulance crews so that even the driver could perform emergency medical services. In 1974, the Albert Einstein College of Medicine in the Bronx began a federally funded pilot program to train paramedics. Graduates were certified by the New York State Department of Health. In 1975, the first two paramedic units with certified EMTs went into service at the Bronx Municipal Hospital Center. In the same year, Albert Einstein College opened its Institute of Emergency Medicine to improve paramedic training. In 1977, Helen Shanes became the first certified woman paramedic to graduate from the program. Today, paramedic training continues at the FDNY/EMS Bureau of Training at Fort Totten in Queens, under the supervision of the New York City Fire Department.

Paramedics in New York City are trained at the FDNY/EMS
Bureau of Training at Fort Totten in Queens.

paramedics in the performance of more advanced lifesaving procedures. Today the paramedic is well versed in medical procedures, and there has been a dramatic decrease in the number of fatalities during transport to the emergency room.

What Makes a Good Paramedic?

Paramedics don't live the quiet life of office workers, and they must make life-and-death decisions in very chaotic circumstances. So you would expect that such a job would require a very unique personality. The occupation of paramedic requires many, if not most, of the following personal attributes:

- You should be an independent thinker.
- You should be able to keep a cool head, especially in an emergency.
- You should not be afraid of seeing a lot of blood.
- You should be mature.
- You should possess both physical and emotional strength.
- You should feel empathy toward others.
- You should be able to take command in an emergency situation.

- You should be able to adjust quickly as a situation changes.
- You should be able to work collaboratively (as part of a team).
- You should be able to drive a motor vehicle.
- You should be able to work at night or at odd hours, and work long shifts.
- You should be able to stay on top of your paperwork.
- You should be able to work with a computer and radio receivers.
- You should be willing to update your skills and never stop learning.
- You should be willing to learn about human anatomy and physiology.
- You should have the ability to deal effectively with the public.

A paramedic is a person who is willing to learn new skills for the rest of his or her life, and who is able to adapt easily and calmly to changing situations. It is essential that paramedics handle critical situations without becoming unglued.

What Do I Need?

2

The employment requirements for paramedics have been evolving, but certain requirements are valid for almost all localities. It is important not to have a criminal record. Currently, a person must have at least a twelfth-grade education with course work in science and must obtain college-level certification as a paramedic. The college certification course may include from one to two years of training, depending on the state or province. A driver's license of the appropriate type for operating emergency vehicles is also a necessity. CPR and first-aid certification are also both required. Some localities have their own individual requirements. A thorough medical examination will be necessary. Paramedics need to be healthy, both physically and emotionally, and they need to be alert on the job at all times.

Many two-year community colleges offer initial training for paramedics. Students at community colleges will receive extensive on-the-job learning experiences, working with emergency workers and other health professionals. There will be an equal balance between classroom and practical instruction, and students will have a variety of experiences that develop expertise and enhance confidence. At the end of the course, they will receive a paramedic diploma.

At the college level, students will be trained in the classroom, at the hospital, and in the field, so to speak. Some of the topics studied at the college level are anatomy, physiology, the theory of prehospital care, therapeutic approaches in crisis situations, mental health issues, the legal responsibilities of health care workers, managing crisis interventions, and the operation of emergency vehicles and equipment. Writing reports is also covered at the college level. There is also training in the physical requirements of being a paramedic. Lifting procedures and the proper handling of patients will be learned. Students will learn how to report child abuse incidents, what kind of language to use in working with children, and how to reassure the elderly. Future paramedics are also trained in how to deal with the sensitive topic of death and dying.

The college program will also include field placement, where students will work with expert paramedics. Both here and in the classroom there will be practical training in emergency care and instruction in how to start an IV, defibrillate heart attack victims, perform CPR, suction wounds, administer medications, and assist in child delivery. College programs usually set up emergency scenarios and monitor how the student handles the situation. Instructors may change the parameters of the scenario or introduce new problems so that the student has to think and act quickly. For example, in simulated emergencies, one person may complain of pain in the stomach whereas another may complain of pain in the chest. The student needs to know how to react in either case. The student will also be trained in crisis interventions, such as suicide prevention and dealing with drug addiction. Students may take part in mock disasters with other groups like local fire and police departments. Paramedics need to understand that in crisis situations there are usually other

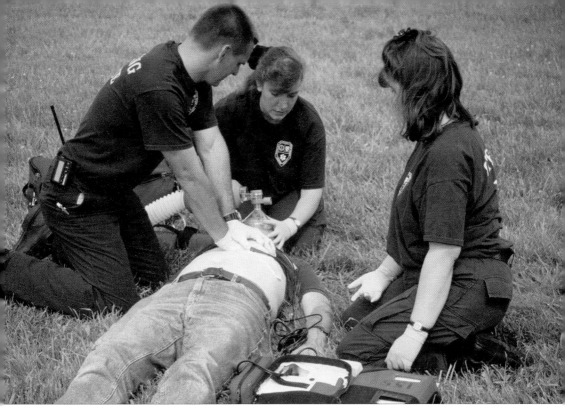
It is essential that paramedics be thoroughly trained in CPR.

people around, and they need to know how to interact and work cooperatively with these other emergency services.

During training, students will have the opportunity to talk to a counselor if they are feeling stressed or overwhelmed by some of the situations they have encountered. Paramedic training may be the first time that the student has ever dealt with a mangled body or seen a dead person.

A Paramedic's Day

Paramedics have been known to deal with up to eight or more patients in a twelve-hour shift. They often have to put in extra hours just to complete their paperwork. They must deal with chaotic street situations, overcrowded emergency rooms, and people in various states of emotional distress. In a typical day a paramedic may have to deal with a person with a heart condition, a number of people involved in car accidents, an alcoholic who has passed out, a teenager who has had a bicycle accident, a person who is bleeding uncontrollably, and an elderly person with lung cancer who can't breathe. There may be time for a quick coffee and a donut along the way, but there is little relief from the steady stream of the sick and injured. The following article from the local newspaper of a small Canadian city describes a typical day in the life of a paramedic.

Work begins at about 7:45 PM. While waiting for a call, the paramedics check the drugs and equipment in the ambulance. At 8:10 PM, they receive their first call. A female has fallen and possibly has a broken leg. The call is not serious—no lights or sirens are required. The paramedics take her to the hospital. It is now 8:50 PM. They take a man suffering from back pain to the hospital. At 1:20 AM, a serious call comes in. An elderly man is having difficulty breathing. *The paramedics race to the address. A fire truck is already on the scene. Just as the paramedics walk into the house, the firefighters hook the patient up to a heart monitor—it's a flat line. Emotions are high. Family members are screaming and crying.*

A firefighter and paramedic begin CPR (cardiopulmonary resuscitation). The paramedic contacts the hospital. Through updates over the phone, the doctor eventually declares the patient dead. The paramedics break the news to the patient's family. The elderly man was in the end-stage of kidney disease with no hope for recovery. Although it's a somewhat expected death given the circumstances, the paramedics still find it difficult to lose a patient. They have to adjust to the scene very quickly; they never know what they're getting into.

The paramedics fill out paperwork at the house and contact the coroner's office. Police arrive later and will stay with the family until the coroner arrives. At 2:22 AM, the paramedics leave the house. Within minutes they are dispatched to another scene. An elderly woman is having trouble breathing. Paramedics check out the patient. They suspect she is having an anxiety attack and calm her down. The paramedics take her to the hospital. In the ambulance, the paramedics discover the woman is going through personal problems. At the hospital, the paramedics fill out paperwork again. They arrive back at 4:00 AM. Ten minutes later, they're dispatched to a car accident. The woman was wearing her seat belt and has only minor scrapes and bruises. She will not be going to the hospital. Police take over at the scene. The paramedics leave the scene at 4:40 AM and head back to the station.

North York Mirror, *September 1999*

Employment

If you are searching for a full-time job as a paramedic, one of the best ways to find employment opportunities is through the bulletin board or placement center of the nearest college that offers the paramedic course. These colleges are kept up to date on who is hiring and what the job requirements are. Some colleges invite private companies and public agencies to come on campus and talk about how graduates can fit into their organizations. Sometimes these invitations evolve into large job fairs where companies actively recruit new employees. You can also learn more about the job market by looking in the telephone book under either

Emergency Medical Services, Paramedics, or Ambulance Services. Employment agencies may have connections with private companies who are looking for paramedics. Depending on where you live, paramedic services may be provided by police and fire departments rather than by an independent agency or a health department, so it might be wise to contact your local police and fire departments for information about employment as a paramedic. Your high school guidance counselor or community college teacher may be able to point you in the right direction. There is also a National Registry exam that you may want to look into.

The Internet can provide you with more information on job requirements in different states and municipalities. Sometimes your skills and qualifications may not be fully transferable between different regions. You may need to verify that your training and your degree are acceptable in the city or state where you are applying for a job.

Most of the paramedics who were interviewed for this book suggested that a good way to begin in this field is to do some volunteer work with your local Emergency Medical Services department. Don't expect

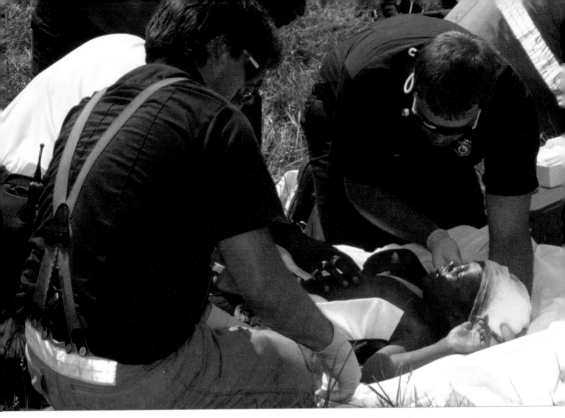

A good way to get started as a paramedic is to do volunteer work with your local Emergency Medical Services department.

to ride in the ambulance as a volunteer, but there may be a support position that you can fill. Many questions about the profession will be answered when you see paramedics in action. And you will be able to decide whether or not this kind of work is for you.

Companies and agencies who are hiring paramedics say that they have a lot of applicants for a very limited number of positions. But do not be discouraged. If you really feel that the job of a paramedic is for you, keep upgrading your skills and sooner or later someone will notice and appreciate your talents and your commitment.

Rick's Story

3

I have been a paramedic since 1975. I am now responsible for providing public information about paramedics. I see my role as promoting awareness of public health issues as well as promoting accident and injury prevention. It is especially important to be aware of children's safety issues in and out of the home. It is also important to train the public in what to do before the ambulance arrives and how to use 911. The role of paramedics is new to the public. Twenty-five years ago they were just ambulance drivers. Today they are far more than that.

Paramedics are front-line emergency medical service providers and are a vital part of the health care system. In many cases a paramedic is making life-and-death decisions with speed and accuracy, sometimes under extremely stressful conditions. At the scene of an accident, the paramedic may orchestrate a rescue with the help of police, firefighters, and citizen volunteers. Paramedics are instinctively alert to general dangers to the community. They are always on the alert for dangers such as fuel leaks, chemical spills, downed electrical wires, fire, and dangerous objects left in public places. A paramedic must be aware of everyone at an accident scene and must be alert at all times. For example, a paramedic may have been called to the scene because a child has had a seizure, but in the kitchen the grandmother is having chest pains from emotional stress. Making the correct assessment, while surrounded by people screaming and crying, is an essential and special skill that paramedics must develop. Paramedics have been trained in the operation of advanced medical equipment to assess and render treatment to their patients.

I feel proud that I chose a career as a paramedic. The most memorable and gratifying moments are when I deliver babies. I have delivered twelve babies in my career, many not under the most ideal conditions—in a car, in the ambulance, or on the couch. After delivering my first, I thought, "That was fantastic!" Some of the most satisfying moments are when we reunite crews with the people whose lives they saved. When paramedics have shocked a person with a defibrillator and that person's heart starts beating again, or when paramedics deliver a baby, reuniting the paramedics with the people who have been helped is a very special moment. Some of the most difficult aspects of my job are the child abuse situations I have had to face. Another condition that hurts and concerns me is the number of people living in squalor on the streets.

I have found that being a paramedic is emotionally, physically, and mentally challenging. One can feel every emotion from anger, elation, shock, and amazement to helplessness and fear. It is important that the good paramedic be a quick decision maker and remain composed under stress. One strength of a paramedic is strong verbal skills and a reassuring manner. You have to be able to tell people that everything is going to be fine, even when you know that things are not going well. As a paramedic, you are a friend, an adviser, a counselor, and a shoulder to cry on. At times you will be a leader and at other times you will be collaborating with others. You will direct the firefighters to where they should be cutting a person out of his or her vehicle, and advise the police on who should be escorted to the hospital. Nothing can prepare you for the blood and some of the other

Some paramedics serve on special teams, such as the Waterborne Ambulance Team of Venice, Italy.

horrible things you will experience. Some paramedics don't have the mental stamina to handle the job. Paramedics can also serve on special teams, such as the Public Safety Unit, Tactical Medics, the Critical Care Transport Team, the Pediatric Team, Mountain Bike Paramedics, the Marine Rescue Unit, and Helicopter Paramedics.

Once you are a paramedic, you are a paramedic twenty-four hours a day. People in the neighborhood will call on you. You will be pushed to the front in any emergency, and your knowledge and expertise will be called upon in any major emergency. A few years ago there was a major subway accident. All units were called. It was summer and extremely hot. People were trapped underground; cell phones would not work. It was 120 degrees Fahrenheit and all the power was out. We had to move quickly and we had to coordinate all our resources. We had to crawl through the wreckage in the heat and darkness. We focused on the people who were trapped and still alive. As always, we treated the dead with dignity.

Being a paramedic is a wonderful job. It is imperative that you have a sense of humor. You will never have two days exactly the same. You get inside the stories that are going on in the news and on television. The indescribable rewards of saving a life, or bringing a new life into this world, have made this profession thoroughly rewarding for me.

Shock

Almost every injury produces some degree of shock. The symptoms may be hardly noticeable, or they may be so severe that the patient dies in spite of the fact that his injuries were not fatal. So what is shock? There are several types of shock, but we are not talking about the emotions you feel when you watch a horror movie! Shock is a medical term, and it means the sudden and rapid loss of blood pressure and blood flow. It may be caused by a physical injury and severe bleeding, damage to the heart muscle, or it may be a nervous reaction to a burn, an electric shock, poisoning, or an animal bite.

Your nervous system has the ability to regulate the size of your blood vessels and, therefore, the amount of blood that reaches various parts of your body. It does this automatically for a variety of reasons—to reduce blood loss from injuries, to direct blood to vital organs, to preserve body heat in cold weather. But the reduction in blood flow deprives parts of the body of nutrients and oxygen, and organs and tissues begin to die. Victims of shock may be nauseous. Their skin becomes pale and cold. Their eyes appear vacant, and their abilities to think and speak clearly are dulled. Unconsciousness and death may follow if there is no rapid treatment.

Susan's Story

4

I have been a paramedic for ten years. I have worked on the road handling emergency calls and nonemergency transfers. At nineteen, I considered nursing, but then I decided to try out this ambulance thing. I've always liked to work outdoors, and I enjoy physical challenges. I was always one to work independently. I completed the twelfth grade and took a one-year paramedics certification course at the local community college. Nowadays it is a two-year certification course. I had to be certified in both first aid and CPR. I also had to have the appropriate class of driver's license in order to drive ambulance vehicles.

I really did not know much about being a paramedic ten years ago, but I know now that I made the right choice. Back then women were only about 10 percent of the force. There are far more women now. I have heard that half the individuals in programs today are women! I felt that being a woman, I had to prove myself both physically and emotionally.

It took me about two years to gain confidence in my chosen profession.

The equipment in the ambulance includes oxygen, a defibrillator, different kinds of stretchers, and a first-aid kit. Always on board are the equipment manuals and policy and procedure manuals and the radio system. Some of the jobs I have been trained to do are symptom relief, defibrillating patients, and administering medications. Part of the job is physical. I lift patients out of their homes, down stairs, and I help extract people who are trapped in cars.

At the beginning of your career as a paramedic, you are usually assigned the most difficult shift and the latest hours. One time I was on the night shift. It was 4:00 in the morning. A woman called 911. She had already been turned away from the hospital because they felt that she was not in labor. My partner and I picked her up in the ambulance. We hit a bump. She said that the baby was coming. Right in front of the hospital I delivered a baby, or I should say that I caught the baby.

On another occasion we were called to an address during the night shift. The woman had tried to commit suicide by cutting her

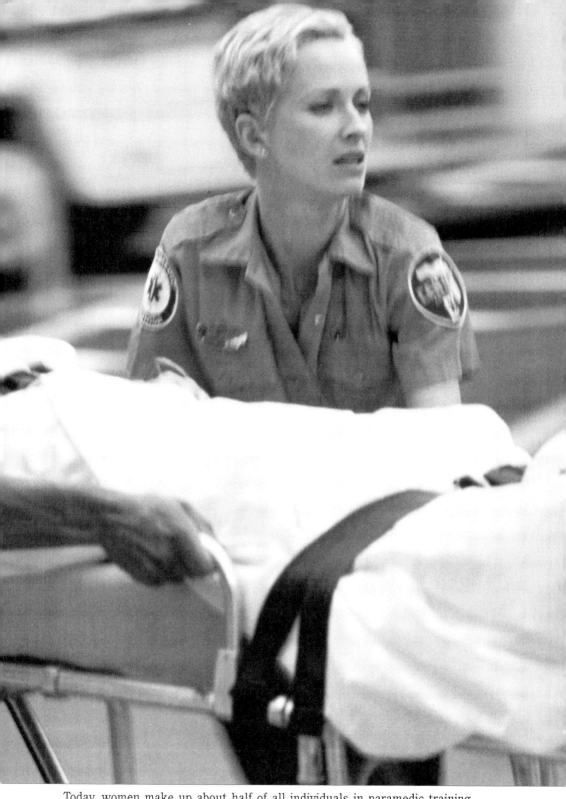
Today, women make up about half of all individuals in paramedic training programs, a dramatic increase compared to past enrollment.

wrists and was threatening to overdose on pills. She was not cooperating. I talked to her. I told her that she could trust me and that I was there to take care of her. She let me bandage her wrists and eventually became calm enough to transport to the hospital. Through the grapevine, I heard that she appreciated what I did for her. Most important to me, I see my patients as people, as human beings.

When on the job, I try to stay calm. It is always important to think about your own personal safety. When at the scene, I stay in the moment. I do not get hungry or tired. Only afterward do I realize what a stressful situation I've been through. One time I was treating a woman and turned my rear to her dog. That quiet dog decided to take a bite. I sat lightly for three days. You never know what to expect!

I feel it is very important to talk out the stress you experience with your coworkers, and in my case I have a supportive significant other. People in the field of emergency lifesaving understand each other and do a lot of listening. I have a lot of job satisfaction. There is enormous satisfaction just from helping an elderly person get back into bed or find something that they need.

My advice to people considering a career as a paramedic is either to try a program in high school or to talk to people in the industry.

Scene Safety

The following statement is from the Basic Life Support Protocols of the Regional Emergency Medical Advisory Committee of New York City. The CFR is the certified first responder, that is, the paramedic.

It is the responsibility of the CFRs to evaluate and judge the scene with regard to safety. Safety factors include, but are not limited to, environmental conditions, the emotional state of the patient or family members, and the contact with potentially hazardous materials and/or spreading of contaminants or disease. Such conditions may be a threat to the health or safety of CFRs, patients, and other persons at the scene. CFRs must also use caution in situations that they are not trained or equipped to handle.

Dr. Gerry Goldberg

5

Companies, counties, and agencies in the United States and Canada recognize the high level of stress that paramedics have to endure every day. Dr. Gerry Goldberg is a psychologist with the Paramedic Employment Assistance Program. The program is designed to assist emergency health care workers with their problems and help them to alleviate their day-to-day stress. The program puts a high emphasis on confidentiality. Dr. Goldberg works with individual paramedics but also provides group therapy through debriefing. Debriefing is the process whereby a professional talks to health care workers after a stressful incident has taken place to discover their feelings and how they are presently functioning. Here is how Dr. Goldberg's job connects with the lives of paramedics.

Historically, as late as the 1970s, paramedics were considered to be little more than ambulance attendants. You might say that in the '70s it was "You call, we haul, that's all." Paramedics were not trained in CPR in those days. Nowadays the paramedic has an enormous variety of skills. These skills are relied on daily as calls for 911 emergency medical care have increased. The paramedics have literally set up mobile emergency rooms in their ambulances.

I have a Ph.D. in psychology, and I am a registered psychologist. I focus mainly on issues related to paramedics. I specialize in job stress, traumatic stress, general counseling, and marital and parental counseling. I also research and write on topics related to work-induced stress. I am housed internally at one of the Emergency Medical Centers, and I am part of the Employee Assistance Program. Anyone on staff can contact me for assistance. I am constantly faced with the problem of helping paramedics to cope with the excitement and unpredictability of their occupation, and their need to get themselves under control while on and off the job. After critical incidents, I hold debriefing sessions with the paramedics.

Critical incidents are events that overwhelm normal coping techniques. These events shake one's gut feeling about the world as a safe and orderly place. The loss of the sense of security combined with vivid, horrifying images of injured people tends to produce strong emotional and physical reactions. For the most part these reactions are normal and usually temporary. Understanding critical incident stress and planning ways to manage that stress will reduce and shorten the impact of the incident. Attending a psychological debriefing headed by a qualified mental health professional is considered an important element in speeding up the recovery period. I tell all paramedics that it is a normal reaction to experience stress after a major incident and that these reactions are usually temporary.

In my job I have to listen to many tragic and gruesome stories. At times I feel that I experience a number of posttraumatic stress symptoms vicariously through the people I talk to. Posttraumatic stress is a psychological disorder that results from experiencing severe trauma. The symptoms may include irritability, depression, and nightmares. In cases where there has been a terrible accident, like a child's drowning, I try to get people together to debrief.

Teens who want to be paramedics should have positive ways to manage stress, such as a regular exercise program.

We talk a bit, and I try to put them on the right track to healing. It is important to prevent behaviors leading to posttraumatic stress disorders. I try to teach paramedics stress-management skills. Some of the things I recommend are the following:

- *Eat regular meals.*
- *Rest, and burn off tension through exercise.*
- *Keep the use of alcohol and medications within normal range.*
- *Talk to people who care about you and whom you trust. Do not bottle things up inside.*

43

• *Attend debriefing sessions.*

• *If the physical or emotional symptoms of posttraumatic stress persist or become overwhelming, consult your physician or mental health professional or go to your local hospital.*

A number of years ago I had a rough day. A child had just drowned and I went to the hospital to help. I conducted a debriefing with the people who had been present at the accident—the paramedics and the scout leader. There was also an accident on the road and three people were killed. Then my pager went off, and I was told to come down to headquarters. There was a subway disaster. All our ambulances were called to the scene. People were running around and there appeared to be a lot of confusion. A triage system was set up so that the most seriously injured would receive priority treatment. Three people had been killed right away, and one person was trapped underground for many hours and then died. I talked with the rescue crews through the difficult hours until 2:00 AM. I then planned a debriefing for hundreds of people to help them with the stress of the

Because of the stressful nature of their job, many paramedics often find themselves physically and emotionally drained.

subway accident. A debriefing for paramedics was also held with the police department.

Everyone in the emergency force needed help with stress. Some had worked for long hours with their attention so focused on their task that they were exhausted and disoriented. Many were both physically and emotionally drained. I listened and helped them to work through their feelings.

In my view the kind of person who wants to be a paramedic is the kind of person who wants to do things well, who gets a lot of satisfaction from helping other people, and who is empathetic to their needs. Paramedics exhibit "compassion in action." And such a person has to be strong. In the midst of chaos, a paramedic must take and keep control.

Paramedicine is a very new field and is still evolving. In the future, ambulances will be equipped with high resolution video cameras that will connect the emergency vehicle to the base hospital. The doctor on the other end will be able to see the patient and further advise the paramedic. New medical technologies and emergency lifesaving procedures will require that the paramedic become an even more skilled medical technician, and the level of emergency services brought to the patient will increase.

David's Story

6

I have been a paramedic for ten years. At present I hold the rank of lieutenant, and I was recently promoted to quality improvement manager. In my family there is a long history of firefighters and police officers. As a young boy, I loved hearing stories about firemen from my great uncle. I became a firefighter first. I had an opportunity to ride with Emergency Medical Services (EMS) and loved the excitement. I knew right away that being a paramedic was what I wanted to do. I then went to a community college to study to become a paramedic.

As a paramedic, I provide advanced life-support services to the sick and injured. I have been trained to defibrillate a heart attack victim, give cardiac drugs, and administer both oxygen and IV solutions. I am also trained to drive an emergency vehicle. On my vehicle I have medical equipment, stretchers, bandaging materials, a stethoscope, neck collars, blood pressure instruments, and pain relief and sedating medications, just to name a few of my supplies.

Where I work, the trend is to merge firefighters and paramedics. In my emergency vehicle, I also carry firefighter's gear, such as air packs with breathable air. One of the objectives of having paramedics with training in fighting fires is that whoever is first on the scene can also assist in a fire rescue.

I remember a 911 call that came from a roadside gas station in the Everglades in Florida. A young woman had gone into labor. We got there just in time, and I assisted in the successful delivery of the baby. I clamped the cord. The child and mother were then flown to the closest hospital. This event was featured on the television show Rescue 911.

On another occasion my partner and I were just getting off duty when over the radio we heard that a shooting was taking place about three blocks away. When we arrived, we witnessed a standoff between the police and a man with a rifle. When we pulled up to the scene, we were informed that a kid had been shot. We could see his feet sticking out of a driveway. We knew that we had to reach the kid, but our unit was blocked in by the police. We had no choice. We grabbed our equipment and put ourselves between the police and the guy with the gun. We reached the youth. He was about twelve. He had been shot in the arm and the abdomen. The situation was life threatening. We took him to the hospital and we later learned that he made it. Thank goodness no one else at the scene was injured that night. My partner and I finally went off duty.

One time I was called to a track meet. A middle school student was running the one-mile event and collapsed. He wasn't breathing and had no pulse when I got to him. We resuscitated him and he survived! I really felt good about the outcome of that event.

I like my job and I know that I am providing a worthwhile service to the community. I have a wife who is also a paramedic. You really need to be able to talk to somebody and tell them your stories. Many times I have said to my wife, "You are not going to believe what happened last night!" Marriages can really suffer from job-related stress if you don't have someone to talk to. You never know on this job when you could be bitten by a dog or attacked by a deranged person or have a needle stuck in you. The stress can build. It helps a lot when your

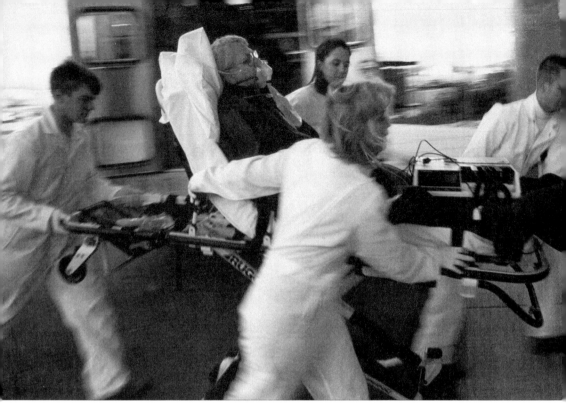

A good paramedic is a person who will work long and hard during many different types of high-stress situations.

actions produce a good result. You feel good when you've delivered a baby or cut someone out of a car or saved a life.

A good paramedic is a person who will work long and hard. The paramedic's job can vary. Two to three percent of my activities do not involve emergency situations. Some people who telephone for our services may not have anyone else to turn to, even if their situations are not life threatening. An elderly person with a toothache or someone who has been suffering with the flu for a week may need our assistance. A paramedic offers

Priorities

What are the three most important things that a paramedic, or anyone coming to the aid of an injured person, must do, and in what order should they be done?

1. First check to see that the victim is breathing. If the victim is not breathing, treating other injuries first will be pointless. Various techniques of artificial ventilation are available to the trained paramedic. Respiratory arrest may be caused by suffocation, drowning, electric shock, toxic fumes, or an obstructed airway. Breathing must be restored.

2. Check to see that the heart is still beating, that the victim has a pulse. Again, if the heart has stopped, treating other injuries will not save the patient. The paramedic may have to perform cardiopulmonary resuscitation (CPR) or employ an electric defibrillator.

3. Finally, control severe bleeding. Loss of blood kills many patients whose injuries can easily be treated if they can be brought to the emergency room in time. Knowing how to apply various compresses, bandages, and tourniquets requires training and experience.

If the patient is breathing, has a strong regular pulse, and is not rapidly losing blood, he or she may be considered stabilized, and there is an excellent chance that the patient will survive if he or she is quickly brought to the emergency room.

compassionate care and connects people with the proper medical services. I do not see myself as an adrenaline junkie. That image is projected on television, but it isn't real.

Conclusion 7

The role that paramedics play continues to evolve. The medical profession has recognized the crucial importance of getting the sick and injured to the hospital as quickly as possible, and it has recognized that the earlier emergency care is given, the more lives will be saved. There is every reason to suppose that in the future, ambulances will carry even more sophisticated medical equipment and paramedics will need more training and skills.

The paramedic is the first medically trained person at the scene of the emergency, and often the first person in authority that the public sees. Paramedics must not simply know what they are doing; they must project an image of competence and confidence. Many people who have been helped by paramedics have stated that it was the paramedic's reassuring voice and cool, controlled behavior that helped them to stay calm.

Paramedics are learning new techniques to help deal with children at scenes of accidents. Paramedics now realize that children need special help with the stressful situations they find themselves involved in, from sickness to violent accidents. It was discovered that children who feel emotional trauma need something to hug and hold on to. As a result, many paramedics now keep teddy bears or other stuffed animals in their emergency vehicles. The following story is from a 1998 issue of the *Journal of Emergency Medical Services.*

Ambulance staff helped a family involved in a motor vehicle accident. The father and son were seriously injured in the crash; the daughter was killed. The father and son wanted to attend the daughter's funeral but were unable to walk. A paramedic crew was assigned as a personal escort so the entire family could be together for the funeral. When the boy, who was in a cast, was transported to the funeral, the crew gave him a teddy bear for consolation. At the funeral home, the crew wheeled the young boy up the aisle to his sister's open casket. Once there, he took her hand, said good-bye, and placed the bear in her hand. "I know you would have loved this," he said.

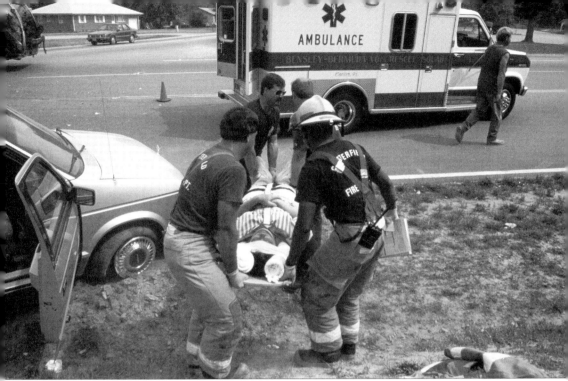

The life of a paramedic is stressful, but most paramedics feel that the rewards of the job are worth the stress.

The life of a paramedic can be emotionally and physically stressful, but almost all paramedics agree that the rewards they receive on the job are worth it. It is not the money that keeps them there, and it is certainly not the adrenaline rush. It is the feeling of helping someone in trouble and making a difference in people's lives.

If you want to help people, and if you are calm, decisive, and able to react quickly under stressful conditions, consider the occupation of paramedic. The following poem was written by Rick, the paramedic whose story was told in chapter 3.

God grant me the strength
to deliver emergency medical care
with skillful hands and a compassionate heart.

Give me the courage and the ability
to render my professional skills
when called upon and lives are on the line.

Help to guide these hands
with love and care
as I bring new life into this world.

Let me ease the suffering of others
from day to day.

Finally, help me accept my fate
and the fate of others
with a clear mind and an open heart.
And by the grace of God I go.

Glossary

carbon monoxide   A colorless, odorless, highly toxic gas.

coroner   A public official who investigates the cause of death.

CPR   Cardiopulmonary resuscitation; any of several methods, usually applied in an emergency situation, for keeping a person's heart pumping and lungs breathing.

debriefing   The practice of extracting information about an experience from its participants, to ease stress and to analyze whether or not the correct actions were taken.

defibrillate   To restore a normal heartbeat through electric shock.

IV   Intravenous; a device for injecting medications directly into the bloodstream through a vein.

57

overdose An excessive dose of medicine or drugs that may cause illness.

palliative Something that will relieve pain or the symptoms of a disease but not cure it.

sedate To calm a person with medication.

shift The scheduled work period for a group of employees.

shock A sudden reduction in blood pressure and blood flow caused by a severe injury. If untreated, shock can be fatal.

trauma A serious physical injury, or the psychological disorder resulting from emotional stress or physical injury.

For More Information

In the United States
National Registry of Emergency
  Medical Technicians
Rocco V. Morando Building
6610 Busch Boulevard
Columbus, OH 43229
(614) 888-4484

In Canada
Calgary EMS
Human Resources Department
Employment Services Division
P.O. Box 2100, Station M
Calgary, Alberta T2P 2MP
(403) 268-2776

Web Sites
Emergency Medical Technicians
http://www.angelfire.com/ok/marvin1226/

EMS Standards
http://www.tdh.state.tx.us/hcqs/ems/faqlicp.htm

EMT Paramedic—National Standard Curriculum
http://www.nhtsa.dot.gov/people/injury/ems

Medic37's EMS Web Site
http://medic37.virtualave.net/

National Flight Paramedics Association
http://www.nfpa.rotor.com/

Paramedic Cyberspace
http://www.paramedic-ems.com

Paramedic Home Page
http://www.paramedic.faithweb.com/

Paramedicine.Com
http://www.paramedicine.com/

San Francisco Paramedic Association
http://www.sfparamedics.org/

For Further Reading

Abbott, Jean T., Marilyn J. Gifford, and
    Scott D. Smitit. *Prehospital Emergency
    Care: A Guide for Paramedics*. Pearl River,
    NY: Parthenon Publishing Group, 1996.
Campbell, John Emory. *Basic Trauma Life
    Support for Paramedics and Advanced
    EMS Providers*. Paramus, NJ: Prentice
    Hall, 1994.
Canning, Peter. *Paramedics on the Front
    Line*. New York: Random House, 1998.
LearningExpress Staff. *Paramedic Licensing
    Exam*. New York: LearningExpress, 1998.
Martin, Scott. *The Paramedic Survival
    Handbook*. Englewood, CO: Skidmore-
    Roth Publishing, 1998.

Masoff, Joy. *Emergency!* Toronto, Canada: Scholastic Canada, 1999.

Rudman, Jack. *Emergency Medical Technicians' Paramedic Examination.* Syosset, NY: National Learning Corporation, 1994.

Shade, Bruce R. *Paramedic Emergency Care.* St. Louis: Mosby, 1993.

Tangherlini, Timothy R. *Talking Trauma: Paramedics & Their Stories.* Jackson, MS: University of Mississippi Press, 1998.

Index

About the Authors

Owen and Sandra Giddens make their home in Toronto, Canada. Owen is a psychotherapist and Sandra is an educational assessment teacher. They have written a number of books for Rosen, most recently *Coping with Grieving and Loss.*

Photo Credits

Cover image and pp. 2, 6, 10, 13, 23, 50 © Uniphoto; p. 17 by Thaddeus Harden; p. 37 by Super Stock; p. 43 by Ira Fox; pp. 28, 32, 45, 55 © Corbis.

Design and Layout

Michael J. Caroleo